SCHOOL DAYS

CARTOONS FROM
THE NEW YORKER

Edited by Robert Mankoff

**Andrews McMeel
Publishing, LLC**

Kansas City • Sydney • London

School Days copyright © 2010 by The New Yorker Magazine. All rights reserved. Printed in the United States of America. No part of this book may be used or reproduced in any manner whatsoever without written permission except in the case of reprints in the context of reviews. For information, write Andrews McMeel Publishing, LLC, an Andrews McMeel Universal company, 1130 Walnut Street, Kansas City, Missouri 64106.

ISBN-13: 978-0-7407-9202-1
ISBN-10: 0-7407-9202-4

Library of Congress Control Number: 2009940826

10 11 12 13 14 MP1 10 9 8 7 6 5 4 3 2 1

www.andrewsmcmeel.com

SCHOOL DAYS

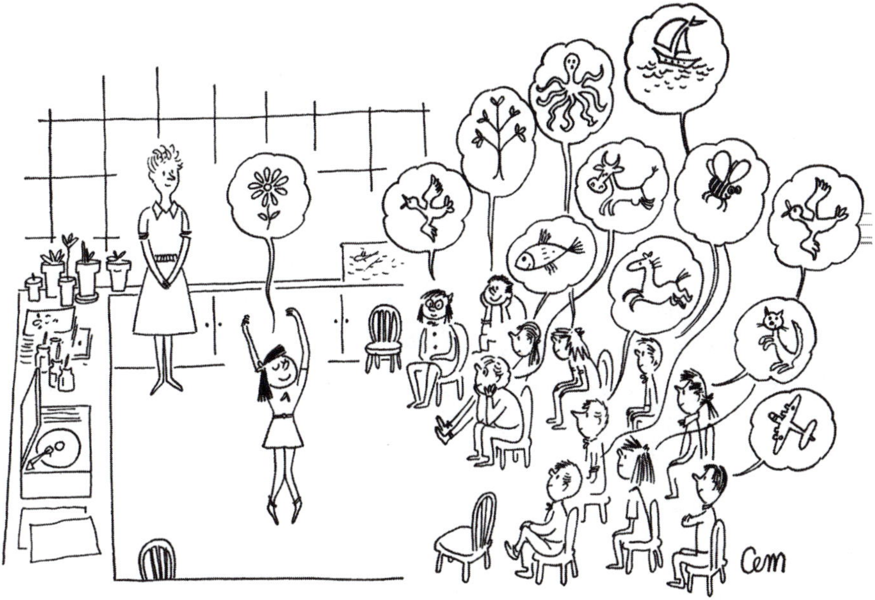
Cem

"And now, ladies and gentlemen, parents, teachers, and friends, the accelerated students of Grade Four are proud to present their adaptation of the Aldous Huxley classic 'Brave New World.'"

"Third grade? Third grade is awesome."

"Very good, Gary: A hero is a celebrity who did something real."

*"And let's remember, children, that the Little Engine
That Could was a locomotive of the female gender."*

"I'm afraid my youthful transgressions may already have eliminated any chance for me to be President."

"Can you believe this is happening to me?
Her scores are very low in self-esteem."

"*Ben is in his first year of high school,
and he's questioning all the right things.*"

"Graduates, faculty, parents, creditors . . ."

"Once upon a time, there was a frozen pizza, and inside the pizza some very bad monsters lived. Their names were refined white flour, reconstituted tomato, and processed cheese. But the worst monster of all was called pepperoni!"

"Dad, I need to dip into my college fund."

"This place reeks of education."

"I'm sick of writing book reports on spec."

*"How do you ever expect to get anywhere
with such a tiny vocabulary?"*

"Miss Finch, my attorney has advised me that I'm not obligated to address the question of what I did on my summer vacation. Nonetheless, I would like to respond."

"I'm having second thoughts about those damn school uniforms."

"It's this marvelous little liberal-arts college in Kansas that gives frequent-flier miles."

"Dad, the dean has gone over your financial statement,
and he doesn't think you're working up to your full potential."

*"It's the whole kindergarten thing, Mom.
I'm alone in there, swimming with the sharks."*

23

*"'What I Did Last Summer', by Scott Sweningen,
as told to Samantha Gerhart."*

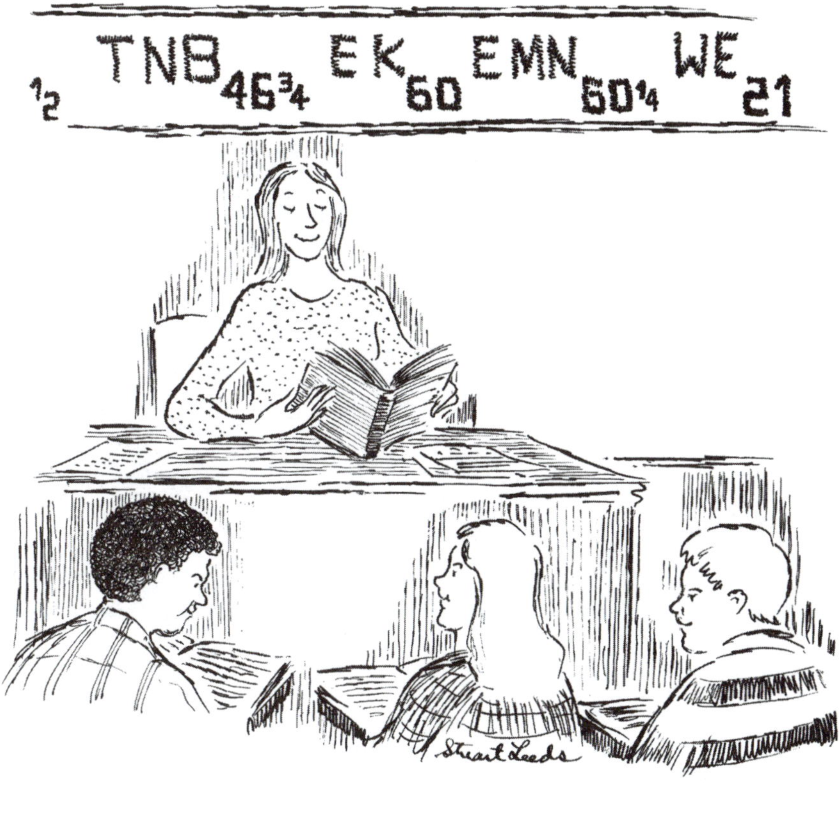
1/2 TNB 46 3/4 EK 60 EMN 60 1/4 WE 21
Stuart Leeds

"I'd trade, but peanut butter sticks to my tongue stud."

"Caroline Dolnick said my dress is a knockoff!"

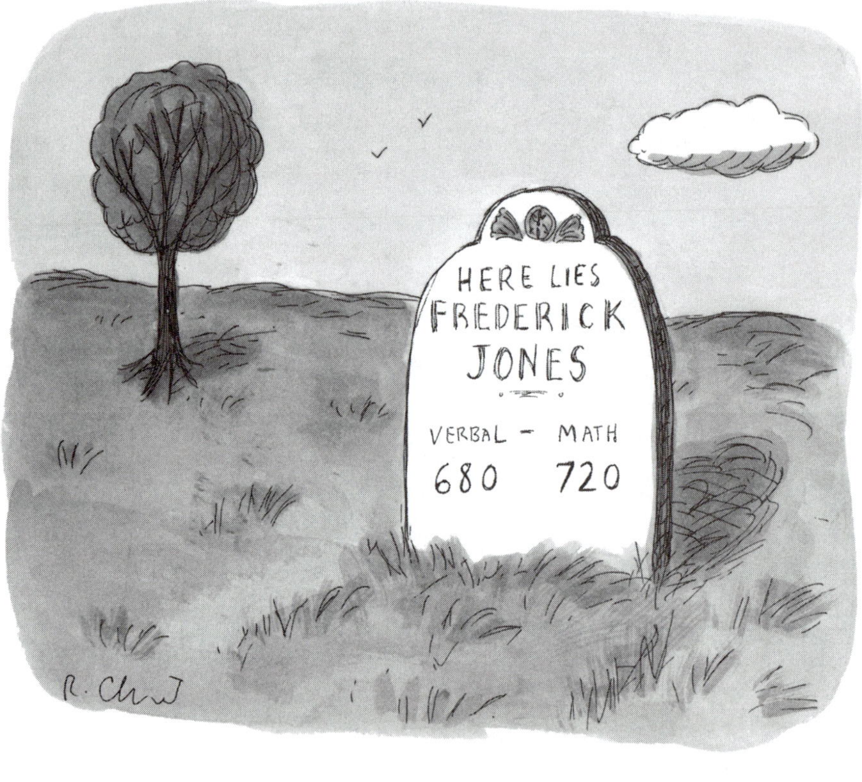
HERE LIES
FREDERICK
JONES
VERBAL - MATH
680 720
R. Chast

"Children, today's story works on many levels."

"I won it for being the most noncompetitive in preschool."

"Daddy's way of helping you with your homework is not to help you."

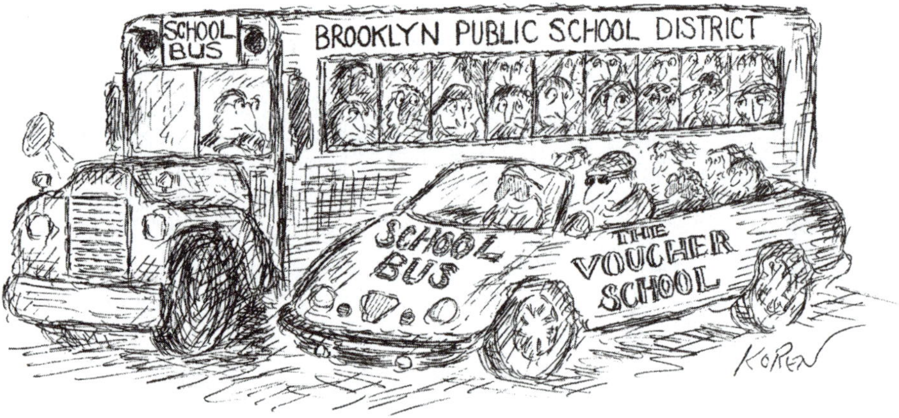
SCHOOL BUS
BROOKLYN PUBLIC SCHOOL DISTRICT
SCHOOL BUS
THE VOUCHER SCHOOL
KOREN

"Todd has been an eager participant in our sex-education program."

"And I'd recommend this book to anyone in the market for a free plush toy."

"I'll pencil you in for recess."

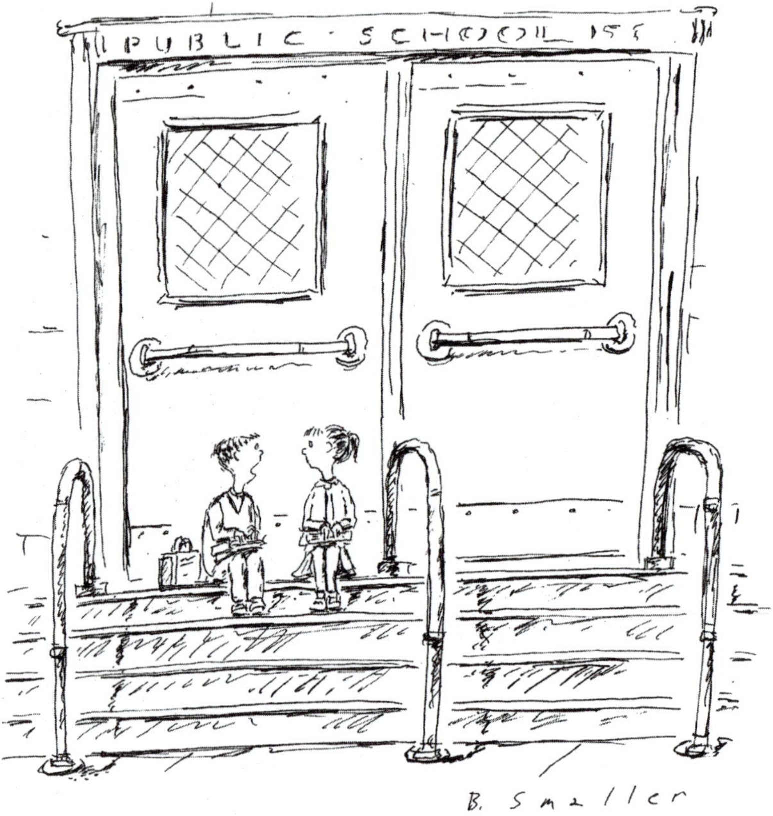
PUBLIC SCHOOL 155
B. Smaller

"O.K., here I am in the fourth grade, but is that really what I want to be doing with my life?"

"I thought it had a pretty good story and interesting characters, but I really didn't like the font."

"Actually, I'm hoping what I'm going to be when I grow up hasn't been invented yet."

*"Thank you, but I've already provided
for my children's college education."*

*"And this is Daniel, who is busy
working toward his degree in money."*

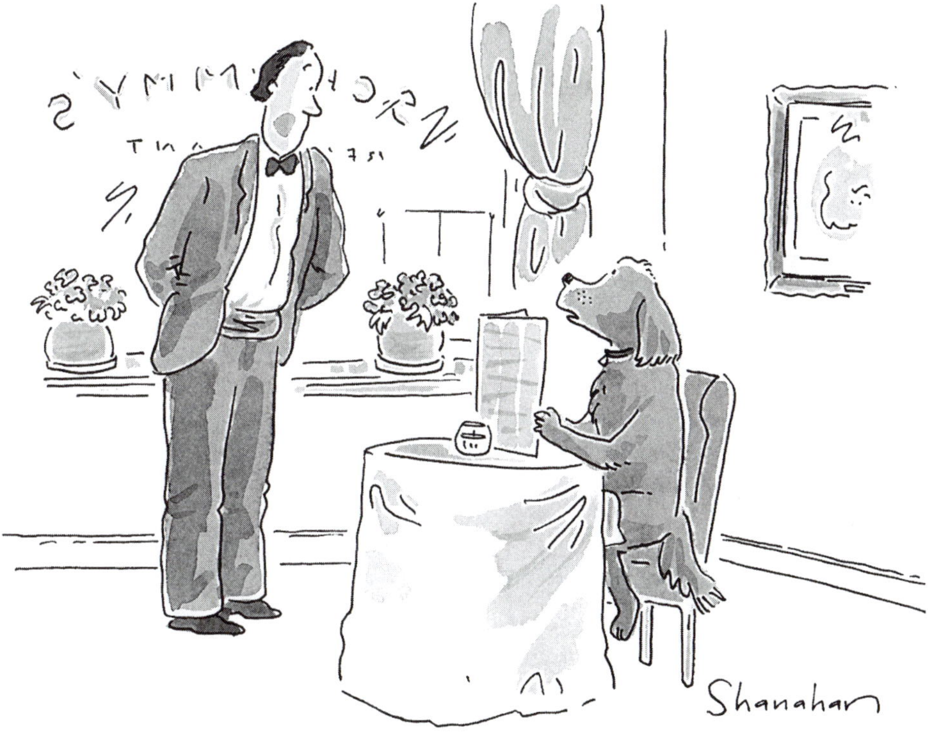
Shanahan

"Is the homework fresh?"

IN A JUST WORLD

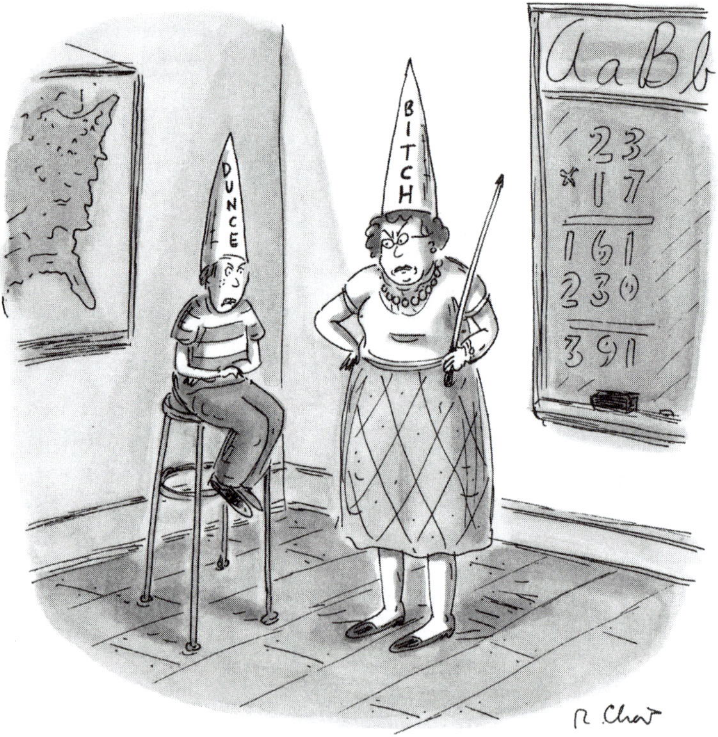
DUNCE
BITCH
AaBb
23
17
161
230
391
R. Chast

"Don't cry, Mom. Lots of parents have children who didn't get into their first-choice college, and they went on to live happy, fulfilled lives."

"We're working on reading readiness."

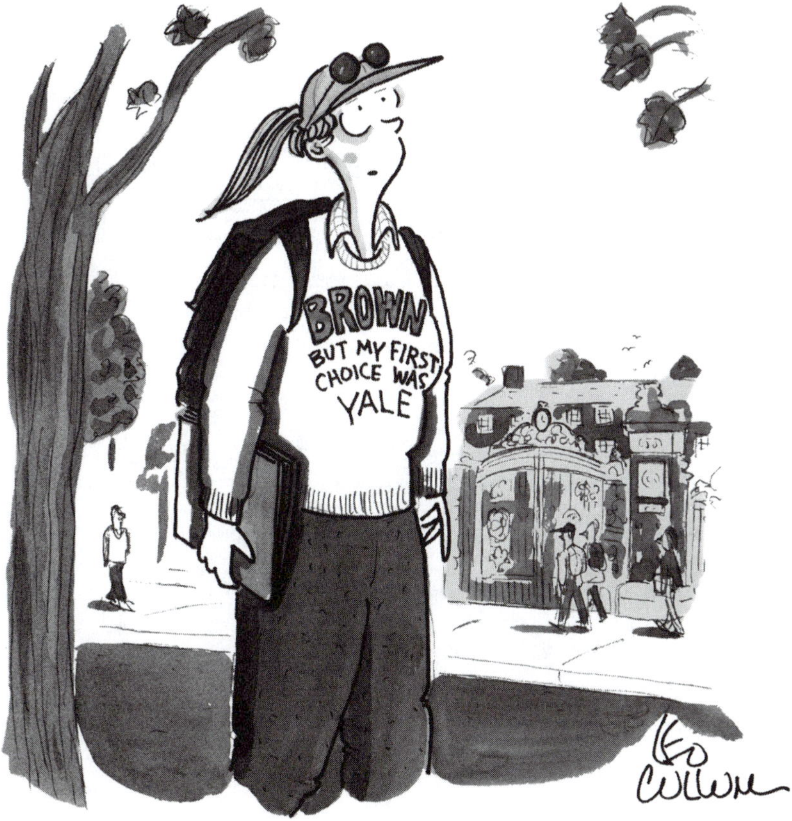
BROWN
BUT MY FIRST CHOICE WAS YALE
LEO CULLUM

*"Now that our last is off to college,
could you tell me who the hell you are?"*

GREGORY

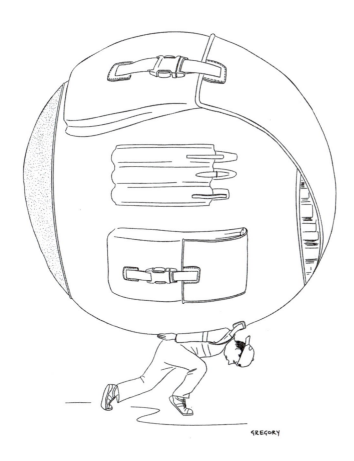

"Summer's coming. How does pre-med camp sound?"

*"I remember you vividly in preschool, when you
played the earth and I starred as the sun."*

"The school could certainly use more hall monitors like you, Peterson."

"I'll pay you double what my parents are giving you <u>not</u> to tutor me."

"There's my very first school—where I learned how to hug."

"I won the spell-check bee."

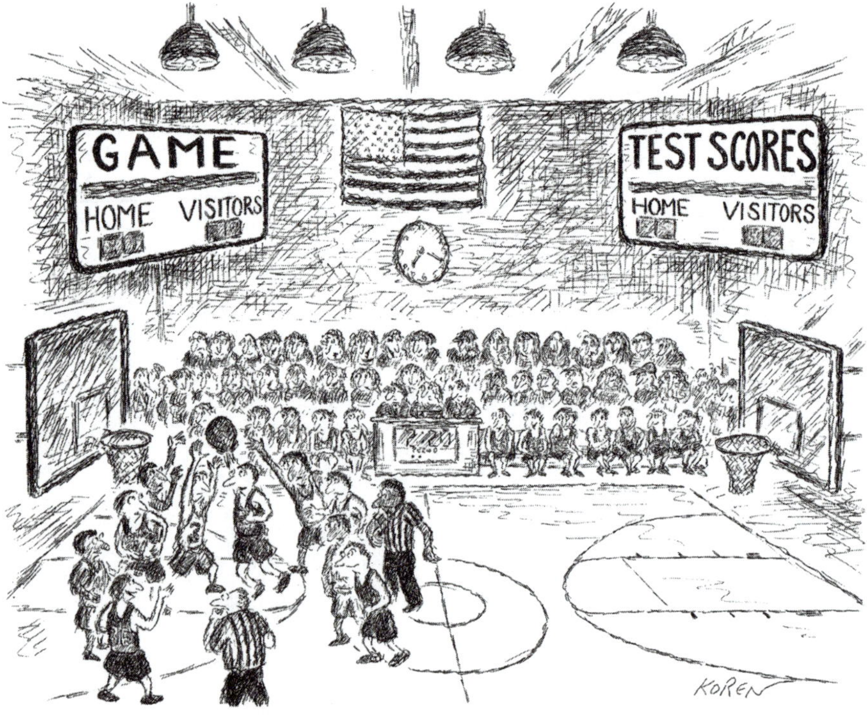
GAME
HOME
VISITORS
TEST SCORES
HOME
VISITORS
KOREN

"Finally, the alphabet is paying off."

"Hang your fading hopes and dreams
on your children's high-school teams!"

"And now Adrian is going to do a
couple of P.S.A.T. practice pages for us."

CREGORY

"We're trying to come up with a less offensive term for political correctness."

"My favorite part of being a stay-at-home
mom is when they're at school."

B. Smaller

"They may be your grades, but they're the return on my investment."

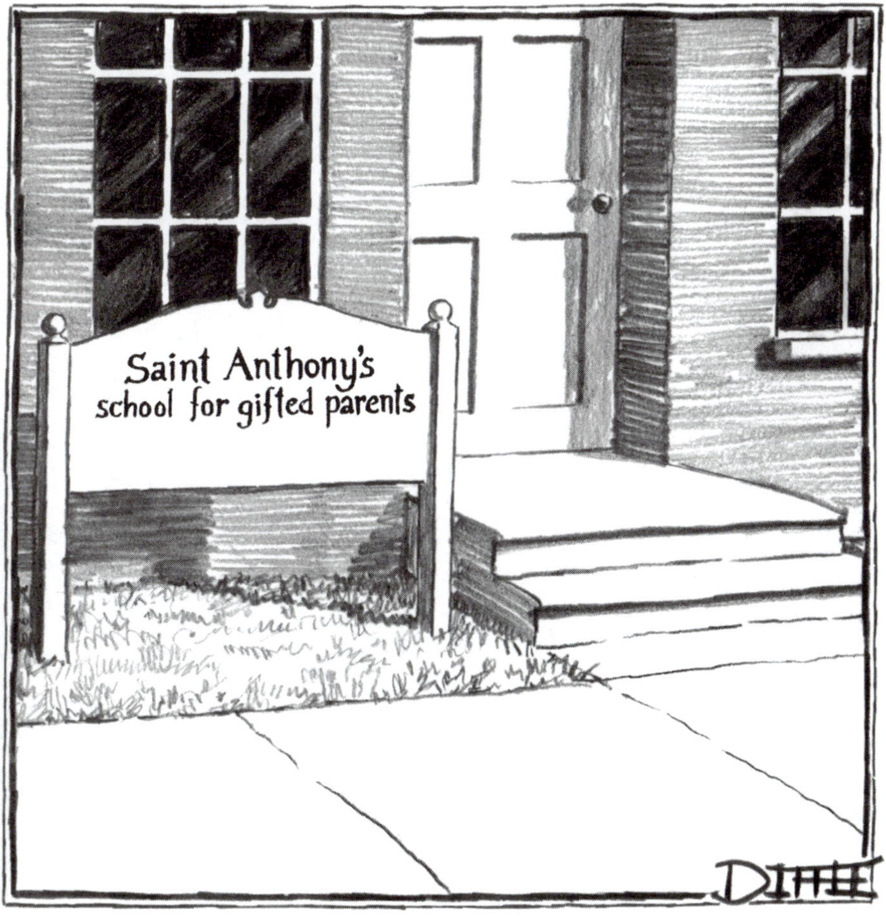
Saint Anthony's
school for gifted parents
DIFFEE

"School's out—academic summer camp is in."

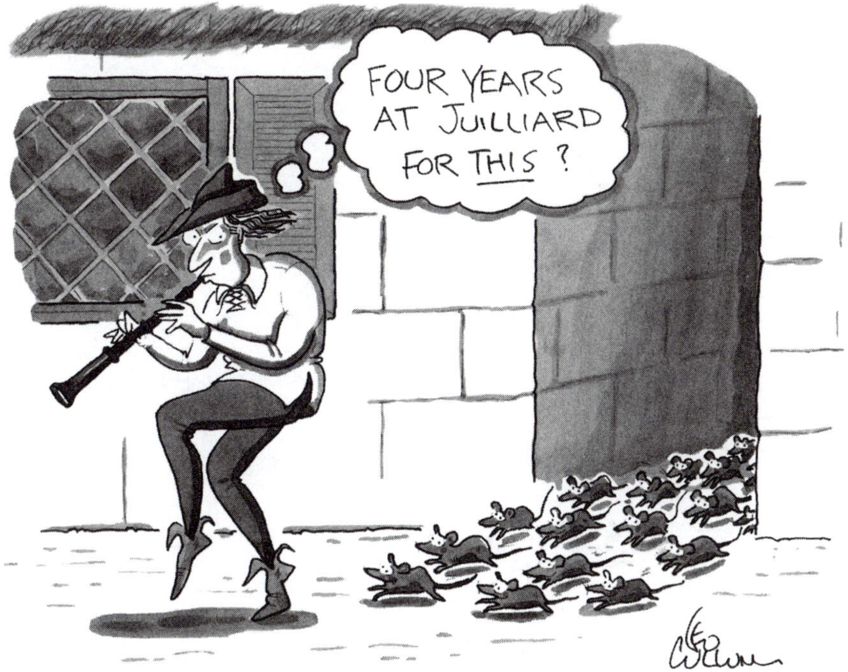
FOUR YEARS AT JUILLIARD FOR THIS ?

"This is our son, Eddy. He's just graduated
from school and is entering a void this fall."

"Don't forget to click 'Reply.'"

*"Dear Mom and Dad: Thanks for the happy childhood.
You've destroyed any chance I had of becoming a writer."*

"We want you to have fun, as long as it's fun that enhances a college-admission application."

"I'm sorry, but I'm morally and politically opposed to hangman."

"My parents never talk to me about S-E-X—all they talk about is S-A-Ts."

"How's school? Have you made some cronies?"

"You're moving into a place where all the
parents live well and all the kids test well."

"Please don't be offended if I consult additional sources of information."

"*The feds have authorized me to leave your child behind.*"

"I didn't go anywhere this summer. I was home-camped."

"Unfortunately, the urine test counted for half of the grade."

"My first-choice college should have lots of closet space."

"Do you have any picture books that could
help a child understand tort reform?"

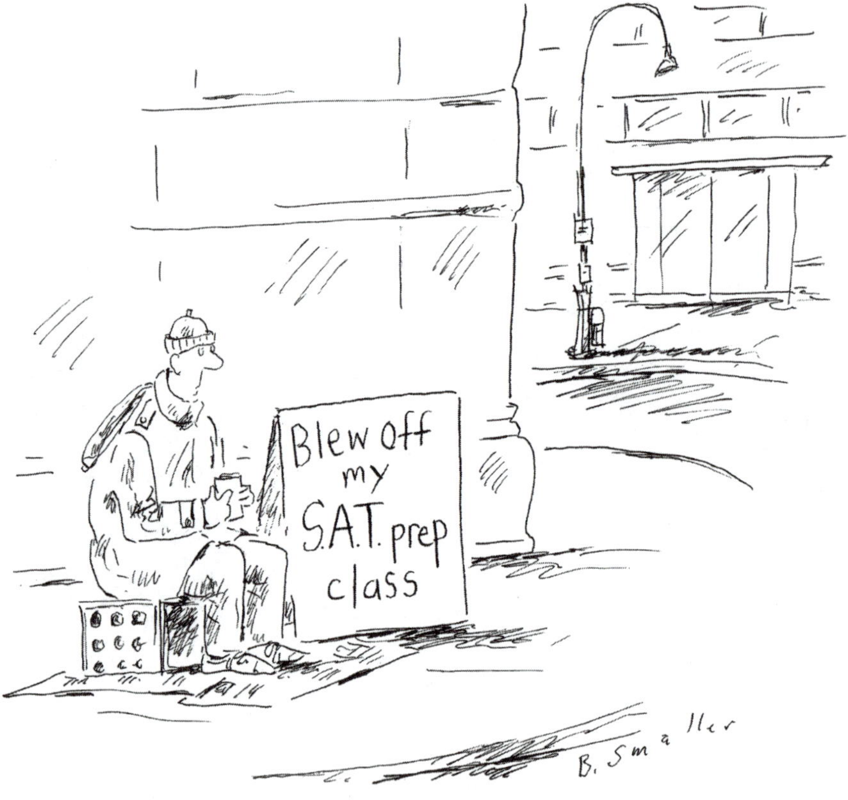
Blew off my S.A.T. prep class
B. Smaller

"What if we stow the 'Star Wars' crap for five seconds,
Timmy, and get to the geometry?"

*"So he got a trophy for good sportsmanship—
that doesn't mean he won't go to law school."*

*"My parents have decided to homeschool me,
but they haven't decided which home."*

"I wonder, Cyndee, whether your parents are aware of this week's spelling of your name."

"He's deliciously old school."

2nd PERIOD OPEN-MIKE PHYSICS

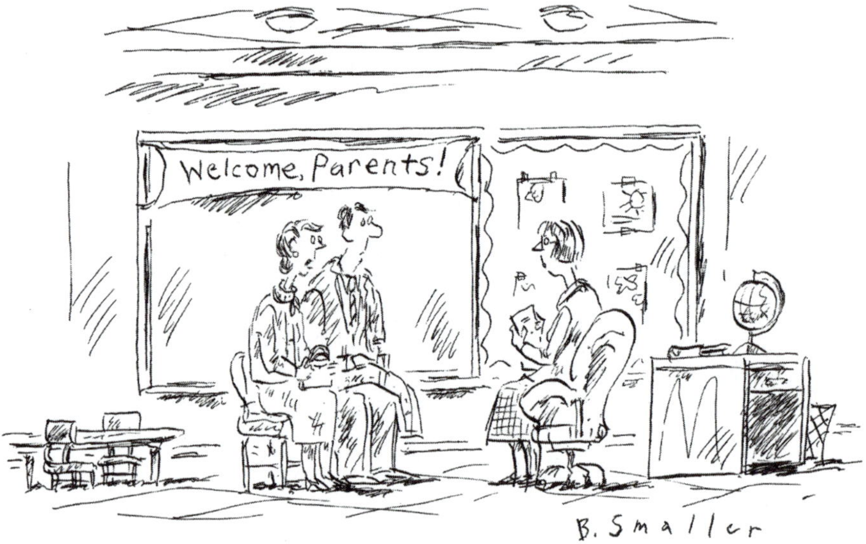
Welcome, Parents!
B. Smaller

"Andy plays perfectly well with others—
it's others who don't play well with Andy."

"What did you learn in school today that I'd object to?"

"It's a lot of pressure on me not to pressure him."

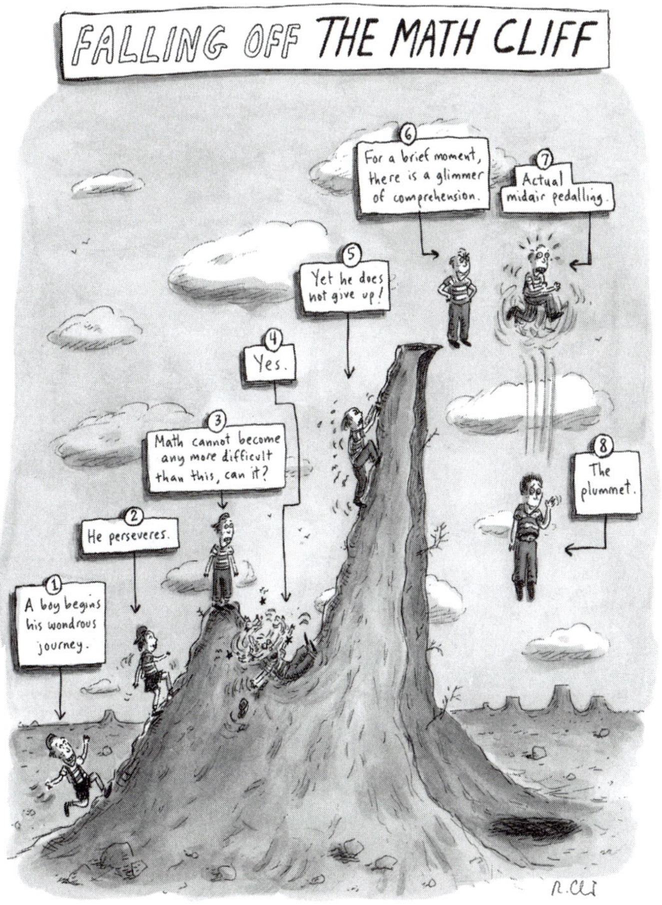
FALLING OFF THE MATH CLIFF
1 A boy begins his wondrous journey.
2 He perseveres.
3 Math cannot become any more difficult than this, can it?
4 Yes.
5 Yet he does not give up!
6 For a brief moment, there is a glimmer of comprehension.
7 Actual midair pedalling.
8 The plummet.
R.Chast

"I need you to line up by attention span."

"Your apple was definitive!"

"I was motor-home-schooled."

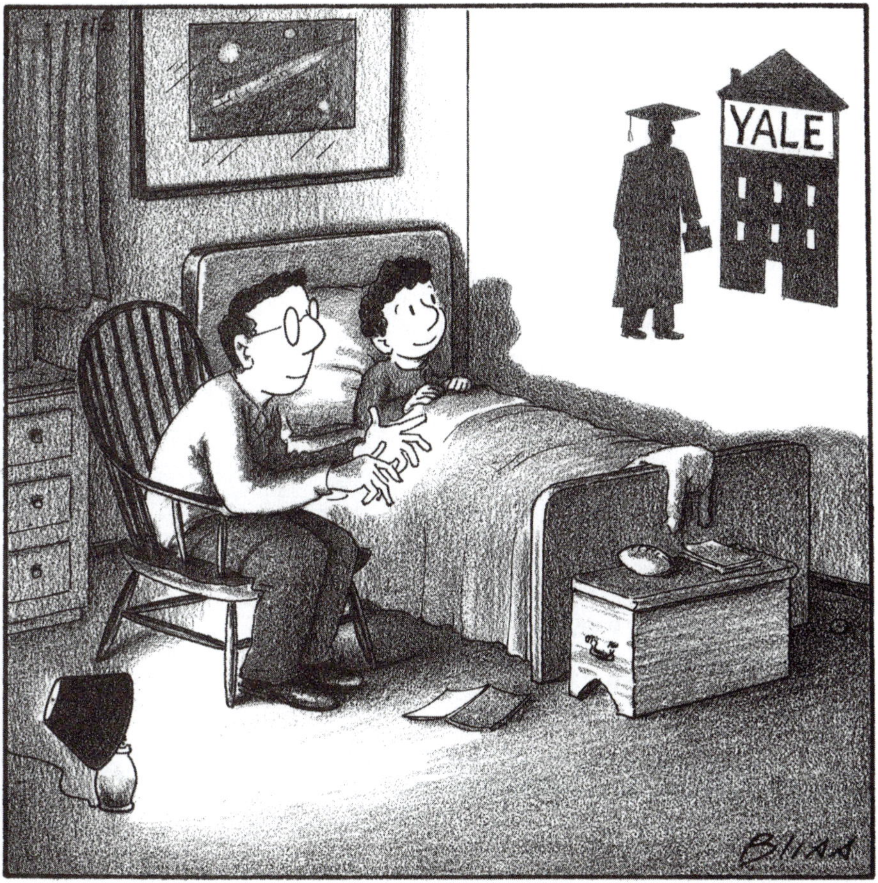
YALE
BLIAN

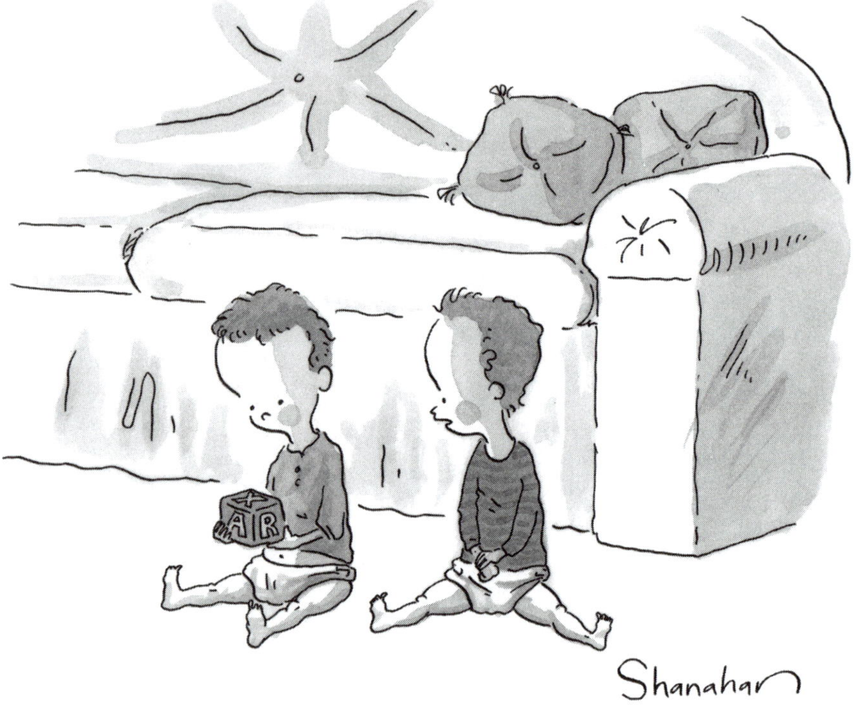
Shanahan

"I couldn't put it down."

"I'm on sabbatical."

"*And just how do you expect to become a made man, son, without a solid liberal-arts education?*"

"I'm holding George back this year because
he's failed to forge a personal style."

"Tommy, you sang along very nicely, but you didn't knock it out of the park."

*"Today we'll be discussing the three branches of government—
executainment, legislatainment, and judiciatainment."*

"Who knows the words to the theme song of the United States?"

"Yes, Justin is a college dropout, but he's a dropout from a very prestigious university."

B. Smaller

"We're done with Baby Einstein. We're on to Baby Bruckheimer."

"Before we go on to division, does anybody want to
share any feelings about multiplication?"

"My parents didn't do my homework for me,
but I did bring them in as consultants."

"If he was really intelligent, he wouldn't limit his applications to East Coast schools."

*"I'm worried about a monster under
my bed and I'm worried about college."*

"I thought I was going to be much more blown away by the Liberty Bell."

"But you can't miss her second-grade first-semester graduation!"

"At this time I'd like to welcome our gold-medallion passengers on board."

INDEX

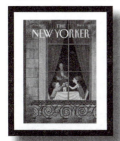

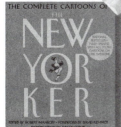

To purchase custom cartoon books and framed prints of cartoons and covers,
or to license cartoons for use in periodicals, Web sites, or other media, please contact:

The Cartoon Bank
A *New Yorker Magazine* Company
800-897-8666 or 914-478-5604
custombooks@cartoonbank.com